# SCULPTURE IN SILK

## Costumes from Japan's Noh Theater

ART CAPITAL GROUP, NEW YORK

Volume has been published in conjunction with
the exhibition "Sculpture in Silk: Costumes from
Japan's Noh Theater."

"Sculpture in Silk: Costumes from Japan's
Noh Theater" exhibition tour commemorates
150 years of Japan-US relations.

Noh costumes reproduced by
Yamaguchi Noh Costume Research Center.
Director: Akira Yamaguchi

Published by Art Capital Group, Inc., New York

Editor: Ashley Milne-Tyte, New York
Design: Steven Schoenfelder, New York
Production: Brooke Marcy, New York
Printing:

All costumes and accessories in this volume are
in the collection of the Yamaguchi Noh Costume
Research Center.

Front cover top: *Karaori* with designs of irises and pontoon
bridges over running water on alternating blocks of color.

Front cover bottom: *Koshiobi* with chrysanthemum crests
on a light blue ground; *Koshiobi* with "scales" triangles on
a gold ground; *Koshiobi* with plum blossoms and checkers
on a red ground; *Koshiobi* with dragon circles on a white
ground; *Koshiobi* with treasures in linked circles on a light
blue ground; *Koshiobi* with shells on a light brown ground;
*Koshiobi* with standing arrows and wave pattern on a blue
ground; Edo Period *Koshiobi* with paulownia and curling
tendrils on a white ground.

Back cover: *Kobeshimi* by Abe Kazuko

## Contents

# Traditional Culture
## &
## the Recreation
## of Noh Costumes

## Kitagawa Zentarō

Although quite a number of Noh costumes still remain from previous centuries, they are slowly vanishing. The reproduction of these costumes was taken on by Yamaguchi Akira of the Azai Noh Research Center in Shiga Prefecture; he studiously analyzed hundreds of costumes for their designs, weave structures, silk thread, dye colors, and construction. At some point, I started to take foreign friends and acquaintances visiting Kyotō to look in on Mr. Yamaguchi and soon started to help him arrange exhibitions of his Noh costumes abroad. The first of these exhibitions was in the ethnological museum in Stockholm, Sweden. There were so many visitors they broke the museum record. Thereafter, for a year-and-a-half, under the auspices of a Japan Foundation grant, Mr. Yamaguchi exhibited his costumes in various museums throughout Europe. Next, with funding from Asahi Newspaper, he mounted an exhibition that was held in the cities of Ōsaka, Nagoya, Yamaguchi, Shizuoka and Niigata, entitled "The World of Noh Costumes: Rebirth of Weaving and Dyeing in Modern Times." This was followed by another exhibition held in Gifu Gunma, Hyōgo, and Toyohashi City called "The Elegant Beauty of Noh Costumes." People associated with these events joined to form The Traditional Culture Forum as Yamaguchi's Noh costumes won high praise both in Japan and abroad.

Noh and Noh costumes symbolize Japanese traditional culture. In the midst of the bustle of our daily lives, an encounter with the traditional culture based on Noh and Noh costumes brings ease of mind. Still, such feelings are fleeting and are not necessarily found in the texts or performance of Noh. In this sense we probably cannot say that the traditional culture of Noh and Noh costumes lives on in our daily lives. It might well be that the connection between our modern life and things of old is slowly fading away.

Noh costumes of the past capture us with their inherent beauty, a distillation of traditional culture not witnessed elsewhere. One might call it the innate character of traditional culture. But is this the only reason for the deep impression they leave? For me, the old Noh costumes speak to us in today's world by transcending time and space through their modern reproductions. Further, the act of creating this specific traditional culture communicates itself to a broad spectrum of people. Universality lies hidden within specificity.

I am not an expert on either Noh costumes or their designs, but they never fail to surprise me with their novelty. The designs simply do no appear old, but actually give an impression of reflecting and even transcending modern artistic values. This struck me when I compared a new Noh costume to an old one. I felt the older, restored costume was more modern than the new one. This incident peaked my interest in the restoration of Noh costumes.

**Atsuita** with a design of axes over a floral hexagon repeat pattern on alternating blocks of color.

At first glance specificity and universality seem to be paradoxical, but careful observation reveals both specific and universal aspects in the designs of Noh costumes. The *seigaiha* pattern (linked concentric arcs) seen in "*atsuita* with dragon roundels, trailing clouds and waves" represents the waves of the ocean. Similar concentric arcs, however, also decorate architecture, for instance, the roof of the remains of the 12th-century Ellenberg in Germany. Similarly, the *shokkō* design, combining octagons and squares, is a design that has been used in Europe and China for many centuries. Other combinations of octagons and squares, for example, can be seen in the mosaic floors of a fourth-century Swiss ruin, as well as on the ceiling of the Vatican in Rome.

For thousands of years people around the world have drawn the same designs over and over, varying in size and color. The time changes, the place changes, the people change, but the designs continue to be created with infinite diversity. One of the beauties of Noh costumes is that in them, the universal blends with that which is innately particular to the costumes. It is possible to develop this idea further since symmetry abounds in the world of designs. Mathematical proof shows that the number of symmetrical designs is finite. In other words, no matter how many designs there may be, as long as they are symmetrical their numbers are limited. People create infinite variations within a framework that is at the same time finite.

Looking at Noh costumes, we feel a world of wisdom spread before us, enriching our spirits. Dyeing, weaving, silk thread, designs, and structure, it doesn't matter which—through the Noh costumes reproduced here we can gain a glimpse of that world. The inspiration I gain from my own encounters with the reproduction of Noh costumes continues to surprise and delight me. ⌘

# CHARACTERISTICS OF NOH COSTUMES

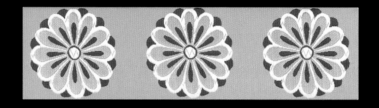

## Kirihata Ken

The Japanese term for Noh costumes (*nō shōzoku*) implies great respect. It is identical to the term for the garments of the nobility and military aristocracy, and it distinguishes them from other stage costumes, like those of Kabuki and Japanese dance, which use the term *ishō*. The weaving-based, Noh costumes represent a highly sophisticated art form whose materials, designs, and techniques combine to form a majestic dignity. This is due to superior weaving techniques, the excellence of the silk thread used, the care with which the thread is dyed, and the infinite pains expended on design. Noh costumes represent the finest in weaving and dyeing in Japan.

"As gorgeous as a Noh costume"—an often-heard analogy—aptly sums up one of the major traits of Noh costumes. Colors interact in subtle ways, their hues transformed by the gleam of silver or gold foil. Elaborate designs are woven layer upon layer, creating a richly sumptuous effect. Even costumes lacking in obvious showiness still have a quality of quiet, inner gorgeousness that leaves a deep impression. The garments used in the Noh theater display the utmost sense of taste and elegance in dyeing and weaving alike.

In general, theatrical costumes have some characteristics that make them different from daily wear; these include a sense of historicism. That is to say, the performing arts present beings who exist beyond the actor, sometimes gods, sometimes other types of people, and their main purpose is to absorb the attention of the audience. Naturally, the costumes serve the same purpose. In addition, Noh costumes contribute a rich brilliance of expression that first and foremost appeals visually to the audience. It is important to note, however, that this brilliance goes deep beneath the surface.

### HISTORY OF NOH DRAMA

How did these costumes come to have such gorgeous elegance? To answer this we must touch on the history of Noh drama. As is well known, Noh was perfected in the early Muromachi period (1392–1568) under the patronage of Ashikaga Yoshimitsu (1358–1408). With Yoshimitsu's unstinting support, this art took on its mature form. Even after Yoshimitsu's death, Noh continued to receive moral and financial backing from the shogun and his feudal lords. The highly cultivated and aristocratic aesthetic sense of such men, nurtured by a thorough grounding in the classical literature of Heian Japan, led naturally to the use of increasingly exquisite and sumptuous garments. Records indicate that gifts were made to actors of gold brocade and damask imported from Ming China. Often, too, when one of the frequent Noh performances was especially well received, the shogun and feudal lords present would rise, strip off their own garments and donate them on the spot. According to the *Tadasu-gawara kanjin sarugaku nikki* (record of the Sarugaku performances on the riverbank near Tadasu) of 1463, in three days no fewer than 237 garments were donated in this fashion. Over time the stripping of each specific type of garment came to be referred to by a separate term, such as "stripping *kosode*" (vest-like garments), and the like. Among the items of clothing so given were many of the finest woven fabrics, including the brocaded *kara-ori*, which was so highly prized that only the shogun himself, and those with his special permission, were allowed to wear it. All these garments, of course, were destined to be worn by actors in performance. This explains another characteristic of Noh costumes: namely, that alongside costumes incorporating elements of the fanciful and the surreal, there were garments straight out of the lives of the upper classes. Surviving examples of some medieval Noh costumes differ in no way from the daily wear of the upper classes of the time. This accounts in part for the Noh costumes being on a par with the garments worn by court nobles and the military elite rather than reflecting the tastes and aspirations of the commoners, as do the costumes of Kabuki and classical Japanese dance.

Supported successively by Oda Nobunaga (1534–1582), Toyotomi Hideyoshi (1536–1598) and Tokugawa Ieyasu (1541–1616), Noh continued to thrive until the Edo period when its position was secured as the ceremonial entertainment of the samurai.

## CATEGORIES OF NOH COSTUMES

A vast assortment of Noh costumes— which fascinate the eye when set against the unadorned Noh stages— survive from the sixteenth century on. These costumes differ from those used in Kabuki in not being identified exclusively with individual roles, or even individual plays. Many garments may be used in any number of roles and plays. The large number of Noh costumes that have been preserved over the centuries, however, suggests how greatly they were valued and that new costumes were constantly being created to specially suit one role or another.

The types of Noh costumes can be divided roughly according to form into (1) *ōso-demono*, or broad-sleeved outer mantles; (2) *kosodemono*, or kimono with single-width sleeves, small cuff openings and overlapping lapels which form a "V" in front; and (3) *hakama*, divided skirts (or pleated pants). There are male and female variations of each type, and among them are some that can be used for either sex and any age.

**Ōsodemono: broad-sleeved outer garments with open cuffs**

**noshi** – loose mantle for men or women with double-width sleeves.
**kariginu** – round-necked hunting cloak with double-width sleeves.
**happi** – men's cloak with double-width sleeves and front and back panels joined by a strap at the hem.

**sobatsugi** – abbreviated, sleeveless version of the *happi*.
**chōken** – dancing cloak of gauze weave in unglossed silk with design woven in gold and colors. Front and back panels fall free.
**maiginu** – women's dancing cloak of gauze weave woven with unglossed silk and an overall design in gold. The front and back panels are joined part way down the side.

**mizugoromo** – plain color traveling cloak in either plain or open weave; worn by men and women.

**hitatare** – suit of matching jacket and long trailing divided skirts. Lined and woven in bast fiber.

**suō** – identical in cut and fabric with the *hitatare*, but unlined.

### Kosodemono: garment with single-width sleeves and small cuff openings

**karaori** – brocade garment for women.

**atsuita** – twill ground garment with either check or brocade pattern, for men.

**atsuita karaori** – brocade garment often worn by warrior-courtiers.

**surihaku** – under-garment of white satin weave with imprinted decorations in gold/silver foil.

**noshime** – men's undergarment of lustrous woven silk.

**nuihaku** – embroidered satin garment worn as outer robe, often with stenciled gold-foil decorations.

**koshimaki** – a *nuihaku* and *surihaku* worn together, the latter exposed above and the former folded down at the waist so the sleeves hang over the hips.

### Hakama: divided skirts

**ōguchi** – plain-colored divided skirts with large pleats in front and stiffened, gathered panels in the back.

**hangire** – broad divided skirts with dynamic gold or silver designs.

**sashinuki** – courtier's pleated pantaloons, gathered at the ankles and worn over *ōguchi*.

**chigobakama** – children's divided skirts.

### Others

**kazura obi** – hair bands worn by women over the wig but under the mask at forehead level.

**koshi obi** – belt sashes.

**others** – hoods, tiaras, etc.

*Karaori* is written with characters reading "Chinese weave," and the cloth is in fact descended from a much-prized woven textile imported from China during the Muromachi period for the shogun's private use. Now virtually a synonym for Noh costumes, *karaori* typifies the gorgeous colorfulness associated with the Noh drama. Worn by women, it combines the sparkle of gold and silver with the hues of many-colored threads woven in complex designs, here "floating" in three-dimensional relief and there bound in a fine, tight weave. As with all Noh costumes, certain conventions are followed in the designs. Small details of the costume give clues about the person wearing it, the most important being the use or non-use of the color red. In general, robes containing red (known as *iro-iri*, literally "with color") are used for young people, those without (*iro-nashi*, or "without color") for women of middle age and above.

The *chōken* and *maiginu* dancing cloaks, in contrast to the polychromatic brilliance of the *karaori*, bring out the beauty of one or two colors. Designs are woven with gold thread on a ground of purple or scarlet, sky blue or grass green. Moreover, both of these types of dancing cloaks are sheer and unlined, so that the design in gold or silver foil on the undergarment of *surihaku* shows through. Both belong to the broad sleeved category, but are tailored in a way not found among ordinary street wear. The *chōken* is also used on occasion to represent the graceful elegance of the young Heike nobleman in armor.

*Atsuita*, another style of small-sleeved brocaded twill garment, display the more serious and powerful side of Noh costumes. Worn by male figures, *atsuita* are used for all sorts of roles—deities, men, goblins, and beasts; young and old, noble and mean—and the designs are correspondingly complex and varied. Like the word *karaori*, the work *atsuita* (or "thick board") refers to a specific kind of woven material. The costume *atsuita*, however, is not limited to that fabric; it can be made from a wide range of weaves, including many colored brocaded textiles with thick float designs and also tightly woven textiles whose twill ground dominates. The designs and weaves express bold intensity for a demon or beast profound quiet charged with poetic melancholy for an old man, whether god or human; military uncouthness for a Genji warlord; graceful refinement for a stripling soldier of the Heike clan; dignity and elegance for the emperor and high court officials; burning resentment for a ghost bent on vengeance.

The *kariginu*, a broad-sleeved outer garment, stems from the hunting cloak worn by Heian noblemen. *Kariginu* come lined and unlined. Lined, they usually are fashioned with gold brocade and used for roles calling for a stern dignity, such as a deity, minister of state, or long-nosed goblin (*tengu*). Unlined, they have a light, gauzy, diaphanous quality, like that of the *chōken,* and are used to suggest the nobility and refinement of the Heian courtiers. Or again, faint and subdued in appearance, unlined *kariginu* may be worn by the spirit of an ancient tree, an aged god, or perhaps the guardian of a forested shrine.

Worthy of particular note is the *Okina kariginu*, a special brocaded garment worn by the smiling old man who represents Okina in the ceremonial play of that title. The pattern used for this garment, octagons connected by surrounding squares and called *shokkō* symbolizes the creation of heaven and earth. This sublime and imposing weave is reserved exclusively for *Okina*. Thus the costume reinforces the special position of the play as a ritual purification and prayer for long life, peace and harmony.

The *happi*, a broad-sleeved cloak unique to Noh, is worn exclusively by men and over *atsuita*. This, too, may be lined or unlined. Lined *happi* of gold brocade are the garb of supernatural beings or of Genji warlords in full armor, while unlined *happi*, like the *kariginu* and *chōken,* reflect the grace of the Heian warrior-courtier.

## COMBINING GARMENTS TO CREATE A COSTUME

In content, production and performance, Noh drama is extremely symbolic and abstract; the same holds true of its costumes. Unlike Kabuki costumes, which often contain numerous explanatory features pertaining to their respective roles, the types of Noh costumes are limited in number and combined variously to express different roles. Each role is created in preeminently abstract terms, and yet with such precise evocation of the essential features that no explanation is necessary. For example, a shining gold *kariginu* cloak worn over white *ōguchi* divided skirts could be the garb of a grand and lofty deity; the same *kariginu* cloak worn with gold brocade *hangiri* presents a majestic *tengu*. *Hangiri* divided skirts worn with unlined *happi* or *chōken* worn over a red *karaori* sprinkled with gold and a pair of red *ōguchi* divided skirts may suggest the imposing splendor of a Heian noblewoman in twelve-layered ceremonial dress (*jūnihitoe*). Again the *karaori* worn snugly draped about the legs (in *kinagashi* style) can serve as the costume of women from any era or station in life. When a *chōken* or *maiginu* is draped on top of this, the outfit becomes the robe of an angel or nymph.

Color and pattern are especially significant in the molding of character by costume. Following the basic distinction noted earlier with regard to the color red, the limited number of Noh costumes takes on almost infinite possibilities in various combinations of hue and design.

## DESIGN PATTERNS

Let us briefly consider some of the characteristics of patterns found in Noh costumes. Patterns divide broadly between those used for male and those used for female roles. Designs of *kariginu, happi, sobatsugi, atsuita,* and *hangiri* are bold, masculine, angular, and often with a notable Chinese flavor. They include Bishamon hexagons (three-pronged medallions), along with gongs (*unpan*), treasure wheels (*hōrin*), dragon roundels, Chinese lions, conches, broadaxes, Chinese phoenixes, flame-shaped drums (*kaendaiko*), swastikas, peonies, and arabesques. The strictly geometric *shokkō* patterns of the Okina *kariginu*, mentioned above, came from China and reflect ancient Indian veneration of the lotus flower.

In sharp contrast, patterns for women's robes tend to be softer, portraying various grasses and flowers of the four seasons. Autumnal motifs are especially popular: bush clovers, pampas grasses, Chinese bellflowers, maiden-flowers, chrysanthemums, and arrowroots. In addition, there are spring cherry blossoms, summer wisteria and irises, winter snow-covered bamboo, pines, and plum blossoms. All of these are traditional Japanese motifs dating back to Heian times and reflecting the traditional Japanese sense of beauty. The preference for flowers and grasses of autumn is evident in the eleventh-century essay *Pillow Book* (*Makura no sōshi*) by Sei Shounagon, filled with exhaustive lists. Furthermore, it is notable that each of these plants is familiar in Japan, figuring in the daily lives of all classes.

*The Tale of Genji,* a 10th-century novel by Lady Murasaki, contains a telling description of the Japanese aesthetic sense, in a commentary on the relative skills of different artists. The explanation goes that however famous or masterful an artist may be, as long as he portrays in his compositions things that ordinary people have no experience of, such as the legendary Isle of Eternal Youth, fearsome monsters from

**Karaori** with design of autumn grasses on a dark brown ground.

some far-off stormy sea, fierce Chinese beasts, or figures of demons and ogres, his works cannot move men's hearts. The painter who instead portrays ordinary hills and streams and scenes from life around him, in a recognizable, soft and pleasing way— say a man who can accurately portray a rough-woven fence—is the truly great artist.

With the above in mind, let us take another look at designs on Noh costumes for women—chrysanthemums on a rough-woven fence; insect cages against an autumn field where clusters of bush clover bloom; scatterings of maple leaves; a vine-covered hut in dewy fields profuse with chrysanthemums, bush clover, pampas grass and bell-flowers, and perhaps a vine of calabash (*yūgao*); wild pinks and wickerwork—each one overflows with the Japanese sense of beauty that extends back to the Heian times.

In this way, costumes for women follow a distinctly Japanese aesthetic. Another facet of Japanese taste may be seen in *chōken* patterns that portray the delicate motions of trailing branches or grasses: weeping cherries, willows, wisteria, kerria (*yamabuki*), bush clover, or pampas grass. A delight in such trailing plants is also traditional in Japan, and such designs come to life on the swirling skirts and fluttering sleeves of dancing women.

Thus the manifold designs of Noh costumes, with the respective characteristics of male and female types, are a colorful adornment to the limited variety of garments used. While, as we have seen, the garments for women reveal a delicate Japanese sensibility, the garments for men exemplify a grander, more robust Chinese aesthetic sense.

Over the past six centuries, Noh costumes have developed along with the drama itself. How new traditions may yet come into being, based on an awareness of the depth of this living tradition, is a major question for the future. ⌘

# NOH MASKS
## AS I SEE THEM

Depictions of theatrical masks from ancient Greece and Rome show wide, open mouths; the words of the poet were to be "voiced through" (*personare*) these mouths. This practice is reflected in many Western languages today. The word "person" derives from it, and the Latin word for "mask" is *persona*.

The ancient masks, with their open mouths and bulging lips, abandoned the subtle imprints of the face as expressive of the individual, of the "personality". One must conclude this from the carved stone remains and images drawn on walls and vases. Generally, whether a mask type was tragic or comic was determined, and the mask type identified, with the aid of hairdos or head ornaments. The delivery of the words, the voice, created the focus of the theatrical performance; it characterized the stage figure and his emotions. The masks were vehicles for the voicing, remaining purely external devices, which were first animated through speech and then developed dramatically into individual fates.

How different, then, the richly varied and fully communicative mouths of the Noh masks! The great expressiveness of these masks is evident as one looks at the mouth. The mouth area, formed in combination with the chin and cheeks (which in the masks of the ancients is lost under a beard), is already eloquently expressive without the aid of words.

Before the main actor (*shite*) puts on the mask, he contemplates its expression meditatively. The mask is his director, so to speak. Even the casual visitor in a museum or the more fortunate person able to hold the mask in his hand, will be astounded by the strength of expression and eloquence imparted by the masks. The shape of the mouth of each Noh mask corresponds with the set forms of the respective roles. In Noh, the words of the actor are not spoken through the mask so as to prevail over it, but with the mask to express its persona. The interpretation of the Noh piece is already set to a large extent by the mask: in the countenance of a good Noh mask that which is essential to the characterization and emotion has already found its expression. The task of the Noh actor is to bring this out and to harmonize it with vocal expression and with the movement of his body, which peaks at the high point of the Noh dance. Due to lack of space here, I cannot enumerate the individual voices of the mask, but every exhibition of Noh masks leaves the visitor with the impression of how effectively the masks seem to be able to shout, whisper, scream, purr, grow silent, groan and fume.

Added to the voices are the glances, the area of the eyes standing for the essence of expression, as it does also in a human face, even though in the Noh masks the living iris, or "mirror of the soul", is missing. To compensate, the Noh masks incorporate the eyebrows and bridge of the nose area into the expression of the eyes, making visible an infinite multiplicity of mood and temper; sculptural details deepen

Gunter
Zobel

and delicate brushstrokes further define the characteristics of repose and energy in each given mask type. The eyes can look out of the mask, then, in a penetrating, or even piercing way, or seem slightly bashful, coquettish or proud; they can stare or look fixedly, fade out or seem blind; sometimes they laugh in a godly way, at other times in a young and artful way.

The flattish female faces, which have a stillness extending out from the eyeballs, are associated with the category of "chōken hyōjō", or "middle expression", which lacks an identifiable single expression and that in the West is easily mistaken for expressionlessness. Just such masks, though, provide the traditionally trained actor the possibility of making the mask appear to come alive by tilting the head upward into the light (terasu) or lowering the head (kumoraseru), or sharply turning the head (kiru). Other masks are sculpted or painted with stylized wrinkles and bumps in the forehead, which often fluently follow the bone structure and creases in the cheeks and around the mouth. The classical Greek division of the face into three sections seems to be reflected in Noh masks as well: forehead, eyes-nose-cheeks, and mouth-chin must combine in expression and fuse into a harmonious whole.

In contrast to the Greek and Roman masks, and indeed to the gigaku and bugaku masks of Japan, the Noh mask does not cover the head, but only the face, often only the central portion of the actor's face. Fundamentally, in Noh, a total illusion should be avoided; the actor should not operate like a puppet, but wear the mask so it is unmistakable as a mask, or so the conventional explanation goes. Actually, the western Noh audience, prepared for the meaningful role of the mask in a performance, often overlooks the fact that from the stage the individual masks appear relatively small and can be viewed only in their entirety, and not in their isolated features. The observant viewer can only surmise which features the shite has employed to create the special nuances of his performance. The theatrical event of a performance is constructed out of a series of separate elements combined into a composite art. The masks achieve their crowning significance supported by the gorgeous costumes that constitute a foundation "throne". As the history of man shows us, vastly differing characters can take their place on a throne. On the Noh stage, the gods of mythology and the goddesses of beauty do in fact wear crowns, the beautiful head decorations called tengan, as a symbol of their immortality.

The carving of a Noh mask, as well as the weaving of a costume, follows an aesthetically developed artistry that builds an architectural form; the costumes can be compared to the "housing" of the individual characters of the Noh. Because of this, their production is not a purpose unto itself, but rather a physical realization of the manifestations and personages of the Noh figures as they have come to be formulated in the plays and masks over hundreds of years. At the time of the perfection of the dramatic form of Noh at the end of the 14th century, the clothes worn for plays were not yet theatrical costumes, but clothing worn by the aristocracy of the time. Only two hundred years later, there was a change; by this time the repertory of the plays and masks had been completed and their number generally set in a canon. Above all, the costumes of the *shite*, the main actor who wears the most meaningful mask, came more and more to be understood as the aesthetic totality and essence of the overall picture and of the individual Noh roles, that were by then well-known to the audience.

On the bare stage, the magnificent profusion of colors and designs of the *shite's* costume functions today as an optically experienced echo of the often-painterly lyrical depictions of nature. It thus enriches numerous texts, generally chanted by the chorus, or by the chorus sharing lines with the *shite*, that describe seasons and landscapes: mountains, trees, blossoms, flowers and grasses. With this, the frequent comparison of the passage of life with the phases of nature surrounding man becomes analogous to a woven stage set of the eloquent motifs.

Even the hand-held objects (*kodōgu*) and the many larger stage props (*tsukurimono*) function on the stage as if they were derived from the costume designs, as if they emerged from an identifiable pattern and objectified it. In addition to the omnipresent fans, the courtier's oxcart (*gosho-guruma*) appears in various forms, and is, particularly in the variant form of a flower cart (*hana-guruma*), a popular textile pattern, appearing also on the Noh costumes. From another point of view, is not the wrapping with red or white cloth around the bamboo structures and frameworks, as well as the decorating of daisies with brocade cloth, a confirmation of this connection?

One should not forget the small sisters of the large costumes, the waist sash (*koshiobi*) and hairbands (*kazuraobi*), which are also a part of Yamaguchi's reproduction plans. The latter work as small decorative ornaments, passing from the center forehead under the mask to the back of the head, and then having the long tie ends fall over the shoulders and back; they function in the Noh as a very meaningful union of textile and mask-carving arts.

Just as the tradition of the Noh schools dictates which Noh plays are to be performed at set times of the year and month, so also set costumes are chosen for these times and roles from a fund of various colors and designs. Thus, the main actor enacts his interpretation of the play through his choice of mask and in conjunction with the music and words, the movement and dance, each time anew, and each time for only one day or evening.

The masks and costumes, with their separate histories of development and their specific aesthetics, so serve the overall performance phenomenon called Noh as to create an experience unique among masked performances today. ⌘

**3.** *Waki* (supporting) actor's dressing room.

**4.** *Shite* (main) actor's dressing room.

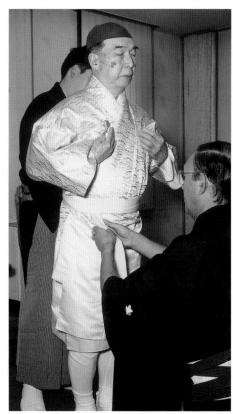

**5.** Donning the *surihaku* under robe. The placement of the belt in determined by the height of the actor and in turn determines the position of the sashes used to secure the outer *karaori* robe.

**6.** Placing the wig on the actor. The hair is combed and then tied at the nape of the neck with a paper cord.

**7.** *Karaori* outer robe is donned so that it falls straight (*kinagashi*).

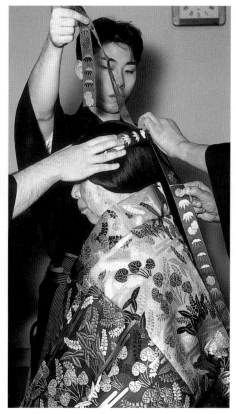

**8.** Tying the hair band (*kazura obi*). The tie in back is placed a little above the section over the forehead and the two ends are evenly aligned.

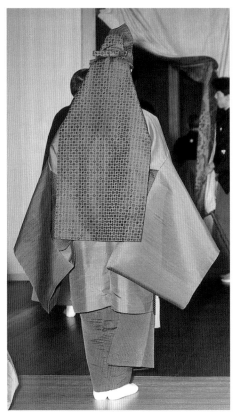

**9.** In the mirror room (*kagami no ma*), the musicians play their warm-up and the *shite* prepares for the first act.

**10.** When the warm-up is over, the curtain is half opened and the instrumentalists walk down the bridge to take their places.

**11.** *Shite's* entrance: When the *shite* says "curtain" (*omaku*), the curtain is lifted.

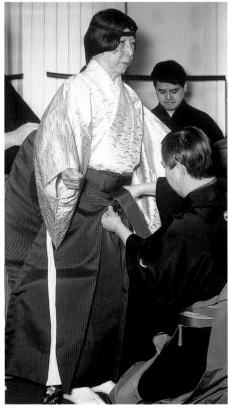

**12.** Exit for the first act (*naka iri*): When the *shite* gets to the third pine, the curtain is lifted. The speed of lifting the curtain differs with the piece.

**13.** Dressing the *shite* for the second act: *Surihaku* under robe and purple divided skirts (*ōkuchi*).

**14.** Donning the *chōken*: The angle of the *chōken* collar is adjusted to that of the *surihaku* and sewed into place.

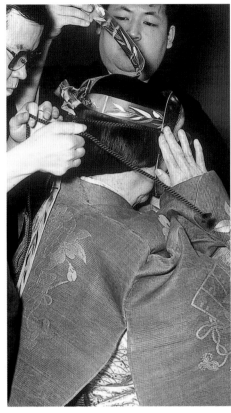

**15.** In the mirror room: Tying the hair band.

**16.** In the mirror room. When the *shite* is fully dressed, he proceeds to the mirror room, sits on a stool, contemplates his figure in the mirror and focuses on concentrating his spirit.

**17.** In the mirror room.

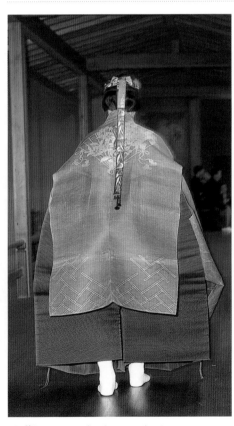

**18.** *Shite* entrance for the second act.

**19.** *Shite* exit at the end of the play.

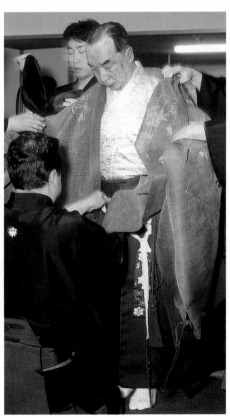

**20.** Stage attendants help the *shite* actor remove his mask and costume.

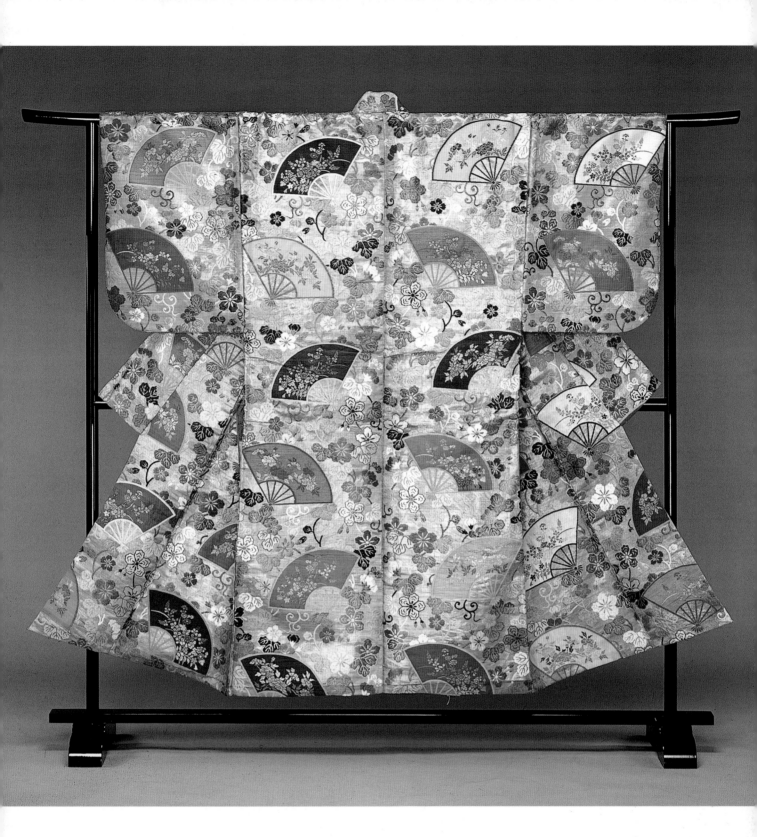

Edo Period **Karaori** with a design
of calabash (yūgao) and fans
decorated with chrysanthemums,
peonies and bush clovers on a
gold ground.

25

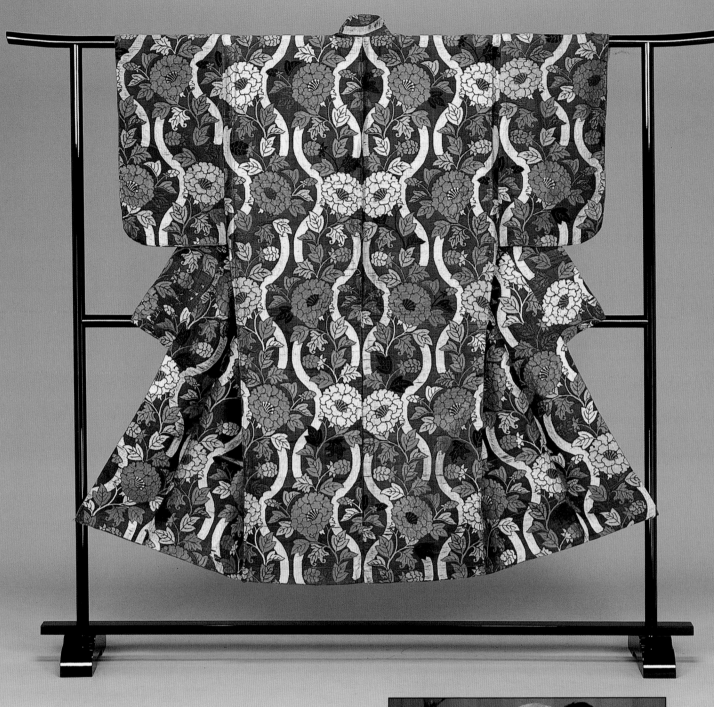

Early Edo Period **Karaori** with a design of peonies and undulating vertical lines on a green ground.

**Yamanba** performed by Shiotsu Akio, Kita School.

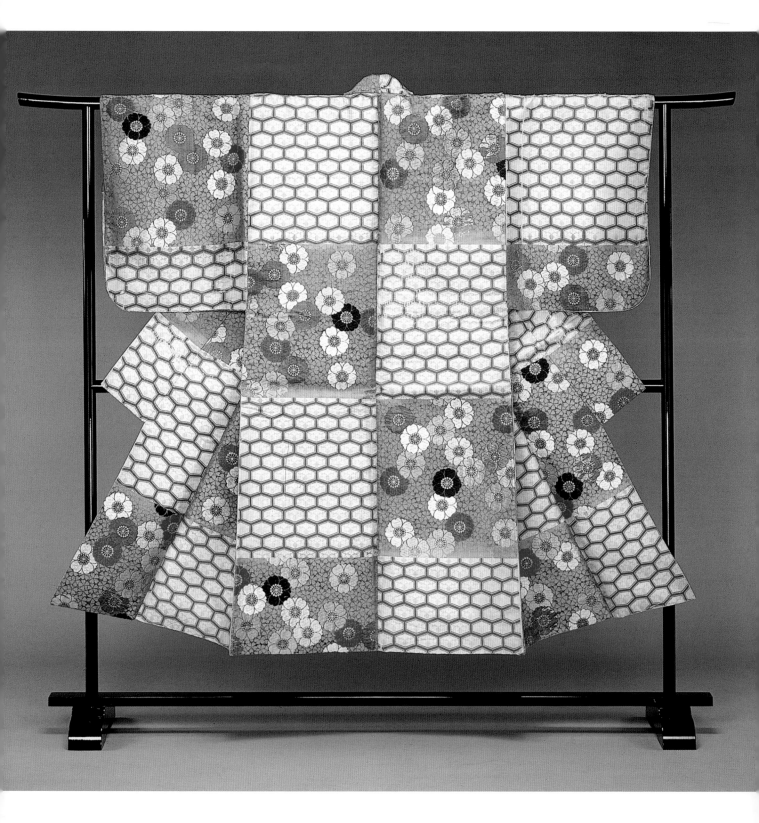

Edo Period **Atsuita-Karaori**
with design of alternating blocks
of hexagonal pattern and cherry
blossoms.

27

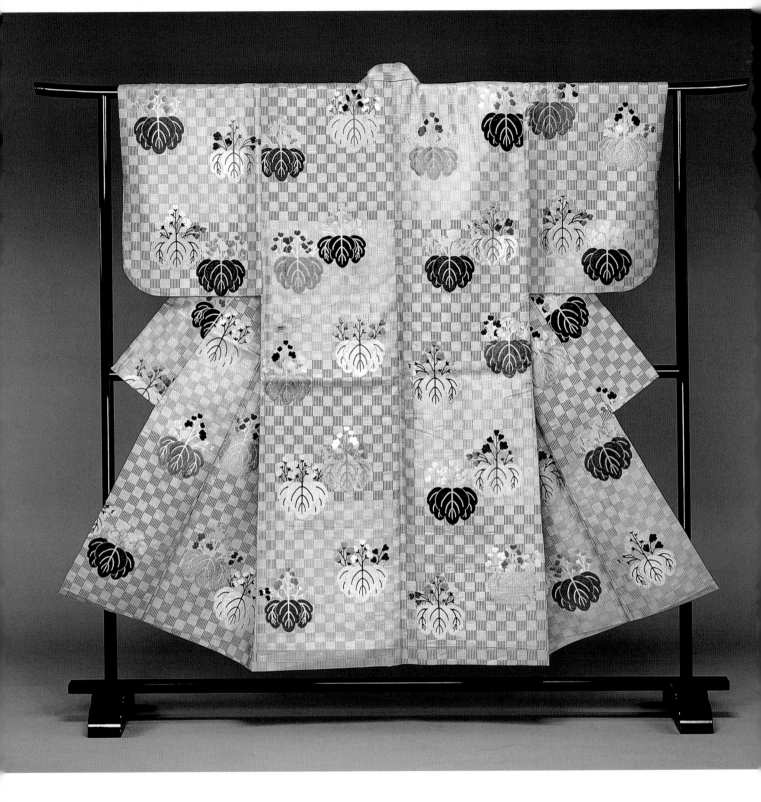

Edo Period **Atsuita-Karaori** with a design of scattered paulownia crests and checker pattern on alternating blocks of color.

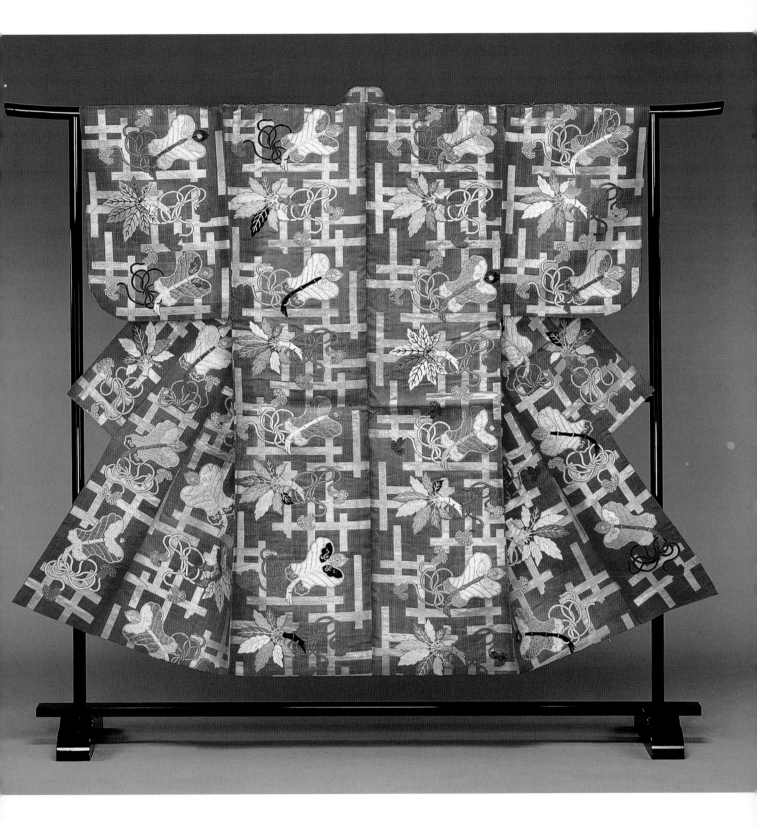

Edo Period **Atsuita** with a design
of Chinese fans and feather fans
and an interrupted well pattern
on a red ground.

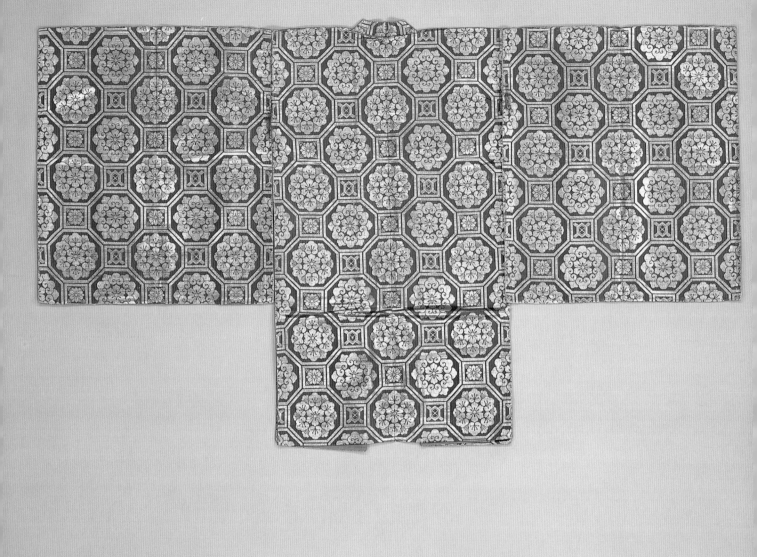

Edo Period **Happi** with a design
of floral crests in a **shokke** pattern
on a purple ground.

Edo Period lined **Kariginu** with a
design of phoenixes and paulownia on a green ground.

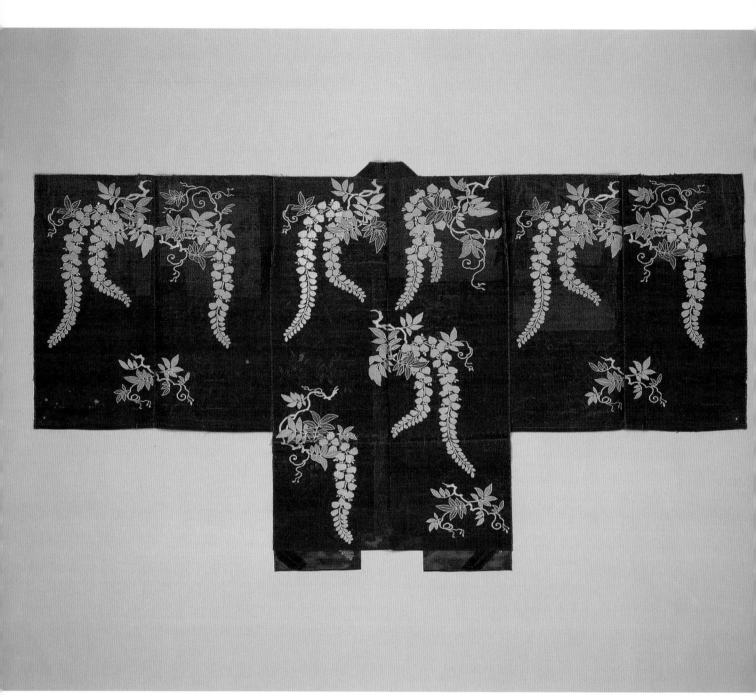

Edo Period **Chōken** with a design
of wisteria on a purple ground.

**Yoshinoshizuka** performed by
Sasaki Muneo, Kita School.

Edo Period **Chōken** with a design
of cherry blossoms with wooden
slat fans on a green ground.

34

**Karaori** with a design of pine and sailboats on a divided gold ground.

**Karaori** with a design of flower carts over a flower-filled linked hexagon repeat pattern on bands of color.

**Yuya** performed by Takeda Yukifusa, Kanze School.

35

36

**Karaori** design of chrysanthemums, cherry blossoms, peonies, and phoenixes over a flower diamond repeat pattern on a white ground.

**Karaori** with a design of chrysanthemums on a green ground.

**Karaori** with a design of calabash (**yūgao**), pinks, and bedstraws (**yae mugura**) on alternating blocks of color.

**Nonomiya** performed by Matsumoto Shigeo, Hōshō School.

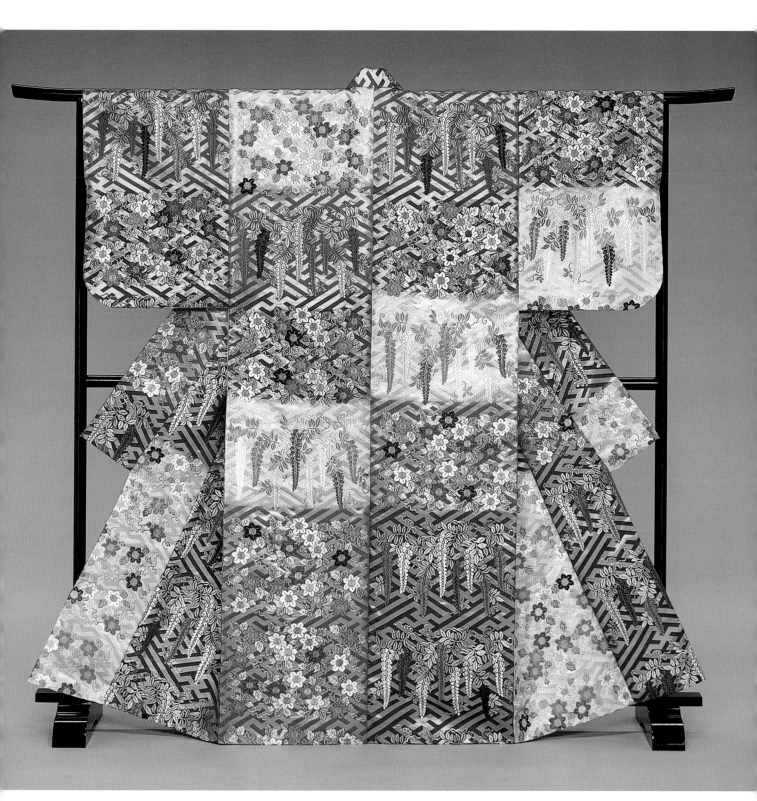

**Karaori** with a design of clematis and wisteria over a key-fret repeat pattern on alternating blocks of color.

**Karaori** with a design of **shōkaidō** (bicolored begonia) over insect cages on a dark brown ground.

**Karaori** with a design of **omodaka**
and hollyhock (**aoi**) over mist on
alternating blocks of color.

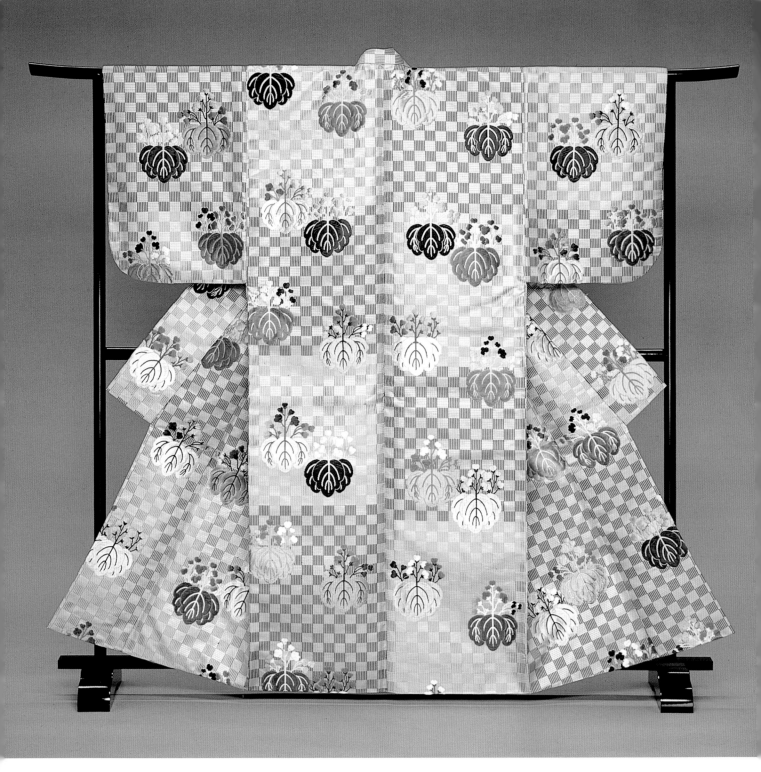

42

**Atsuita-Karaori** with a design of scattered paulownia crests over a checker pattern on a white ground.

**Karaori** with a design of plants, flowers, and flower carts with fence repeat pattern on alternating blocks of color.

**Eguchi** performed by Tomoeda Akiyo, Kita School.

43

44

**Atsuita-Karaori** with a design of flower baskets with a crest-filled checker pattern on a dark brown ground.

**Atsuita-Karaori** with a design of
lilies and trumpet creepers over a
diamond repeat pattern on alternating blocks of color.

45

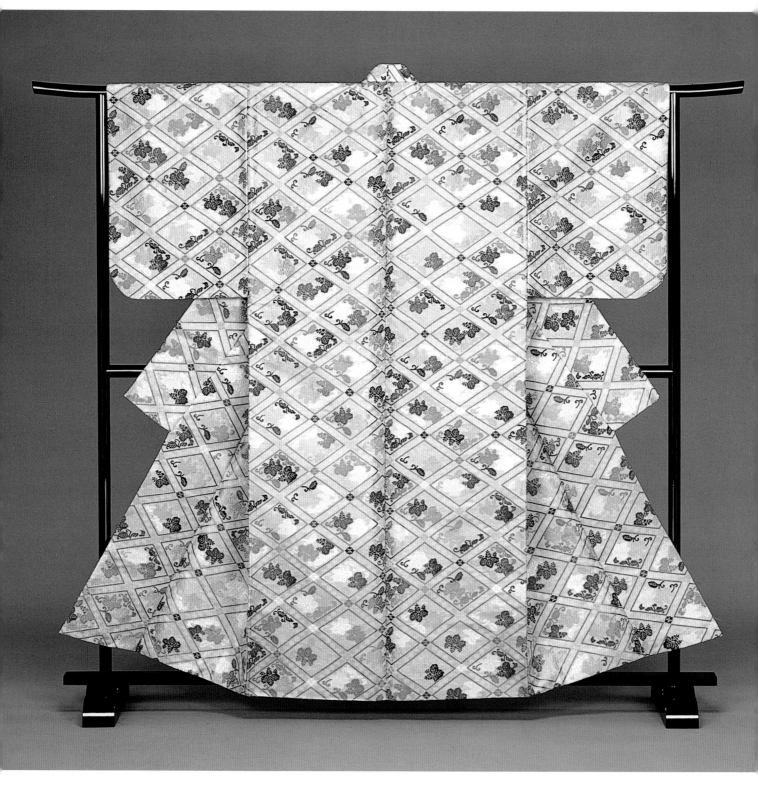

**Atsuita-Karaori** with a design of diamonds containing paulownia and curling tendrils on a white ground.

**Atsuita** with a design of dragon
circles and trailing clouds over
lightening on a gray-blue ground.

48

**Atsuita** with a design of flower crests and curving lines over a "scale" triangle repeat pattern on alternating blocks of color.

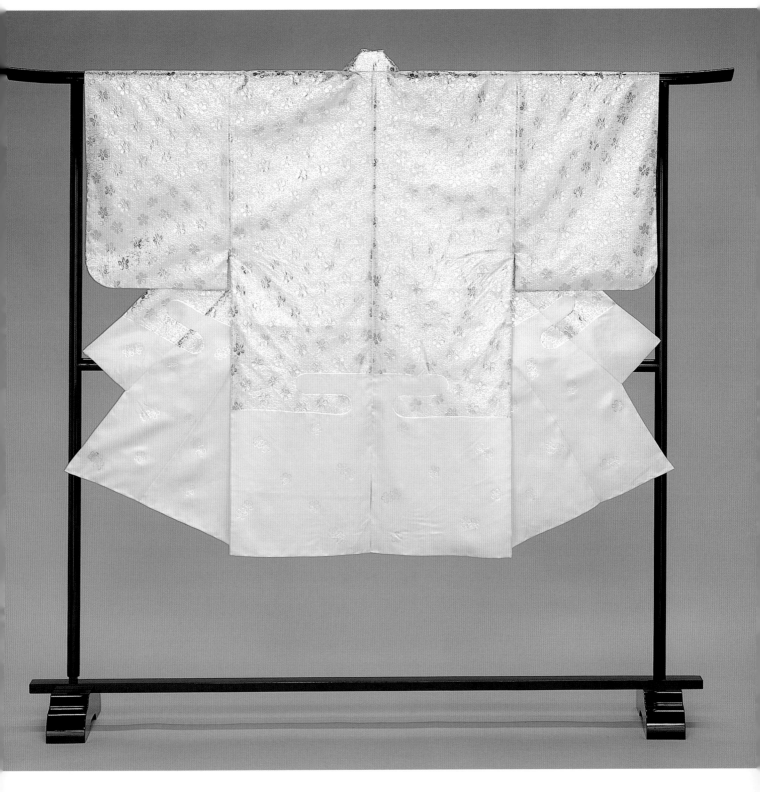

**Surihaku** with a design of cherry
blossoms on a white ground.

**Chōken** with a design of pampas grass and butterflies on a purple ground.

**Kochō** performed by Matsumoto Shigeo, Hōshō School.

**Chōken** with a design of rice ears
and clappers on a white ground.

**Chōken** with a design of wisteria, pines and mist with dandelions on a purple ground.

**Chōken** with a design of flower baskets and waves pattern with scattered flower spring on a blue ground.

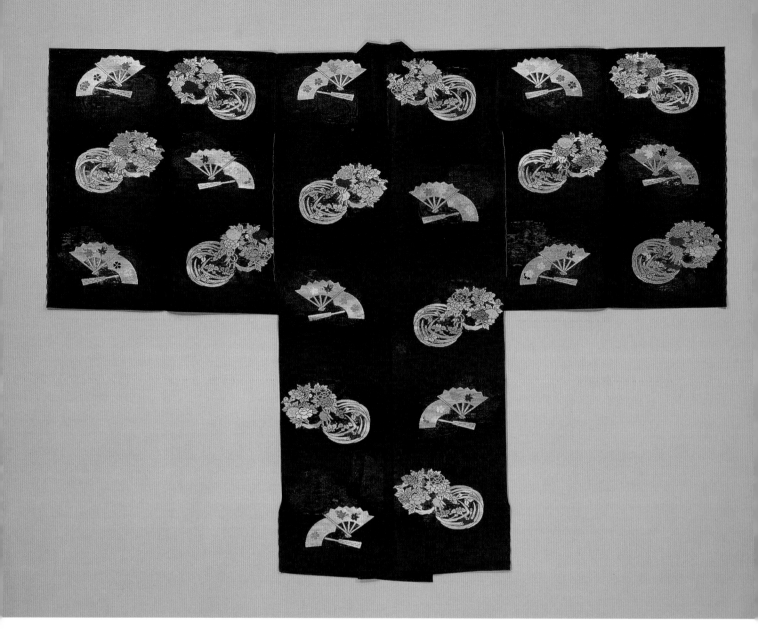

**Maiginu** with a design of flower rounds and fans on a purple ground.

**Maiginu** with a design of chrysanthemums and curling tendrils on a red ground.

**Tatsuta** performed by Kagawa Yasutsugu, Kita School.

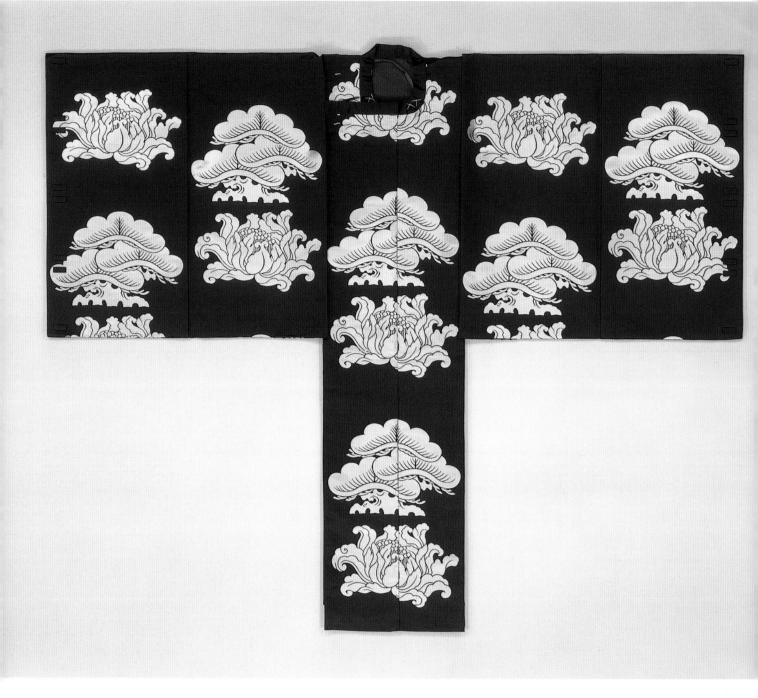

Lined **Kariginu** with a design of three-tiered pines with peonies on a blue ground.

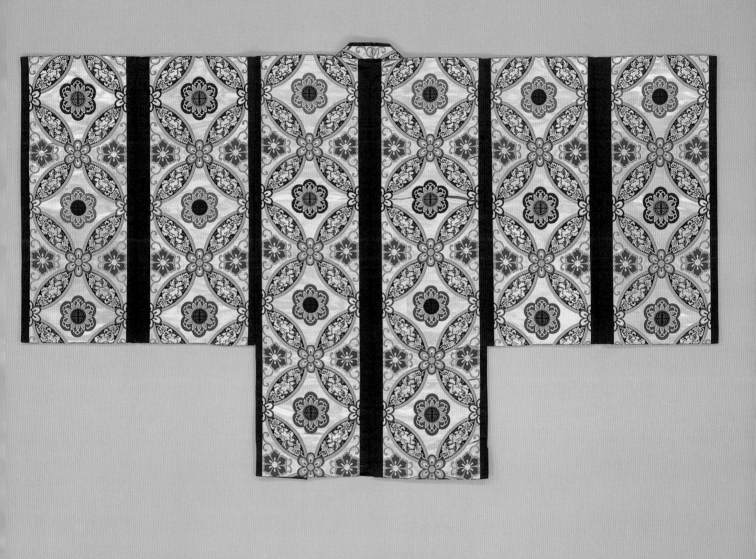

**Happi** with a design of interlocking circles enclosing flower crests on a dark blue ground.

**Hangiri** with a design of standing waves and lightening on a blue ground.

**Hangiri** with a design of
chrysanthemums arabesques
on a blue ground.

Edo Period **Koshiobi** with camellia on a white ground.

Edo Period **Koshiobi** with paulownia on a red ground.

Edo Period **Koshiobi** with clematis on a light blue ground.

**Koshiobi** with autumn grasses on a light blue ground.

**Koshiobi** with curling vines on a green ground.

**Koshiobi** with standing arrows and wave pattern on a blue ground.

61

**Koshiobi** with wheels on waves on a light blue ground.

**Koshiobi** with irises on running water on a dark brown ground.

**Koshiobi** with dragon circles on a white ground.

**Koshiobi** with good luck characters on undulating lines on a white ground.

**Koshiobi** with shells on a light brown ground.

**Koshiobi** with plum blossoms and checkers on a red ground.

63

**Koshiobi** with treasures in linked circles on a light blue ground.

**Koshiobi** with paulownia crests and flower diamonds on a white ground.

**Koshiobi** with pines, wisteria and clouds on a red ground.

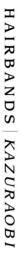

Edo Period **Kazuraobi** with weeping cherry blossom branches on a red ground.

Edo Period **Kazuraobi** with weeping cherry blossom branches on a gold ground.

**Kazuraobi** with camellia on a gold ground.

**Kazuraobi** with scattered rounds on a white ground.

**Kazuraobi** with sea grasses and shells on a white ground.

65

**Kazuraobi** morning
glories and undulasting
lines on a blue ground.

**Kazuraobi** with clematis
on a blue ground.

**Kazuraobi** with plums
and key-fret pattern on
a golden brown ground.

**Kazuraobi** with young
pines and undulating lines
on a dark brown ground.

**Kazuraobi** with wisteria
on bamboo fences on a
red ground.

**Kazuraobi** with leaves and curling tendrils on a dark brown ground.

**Kazuraobi** with snow-laden bamboo grass on a blue ground.

**Kazuraobi** with clematis, chrysanthemums and bush clovers wrapped in folded papers on a gold ground.

**Kazuraobi** with autumn leaves on a green ground.

**Kazuraobi** with snow-laden willows on a light brown ground.

67

# MASKS

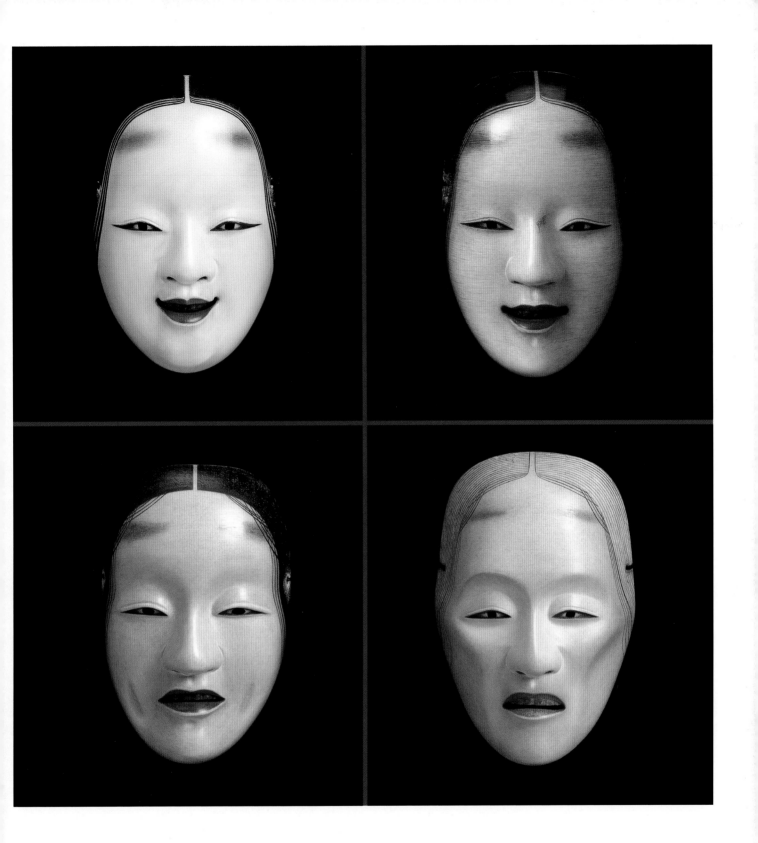

**Ko-omote** by Suzuki Keiun
**Fushikizō** by Abe Kazuko

**Shakumi** by Abe Kazuko
**Rōjo** by Abe Kazuko

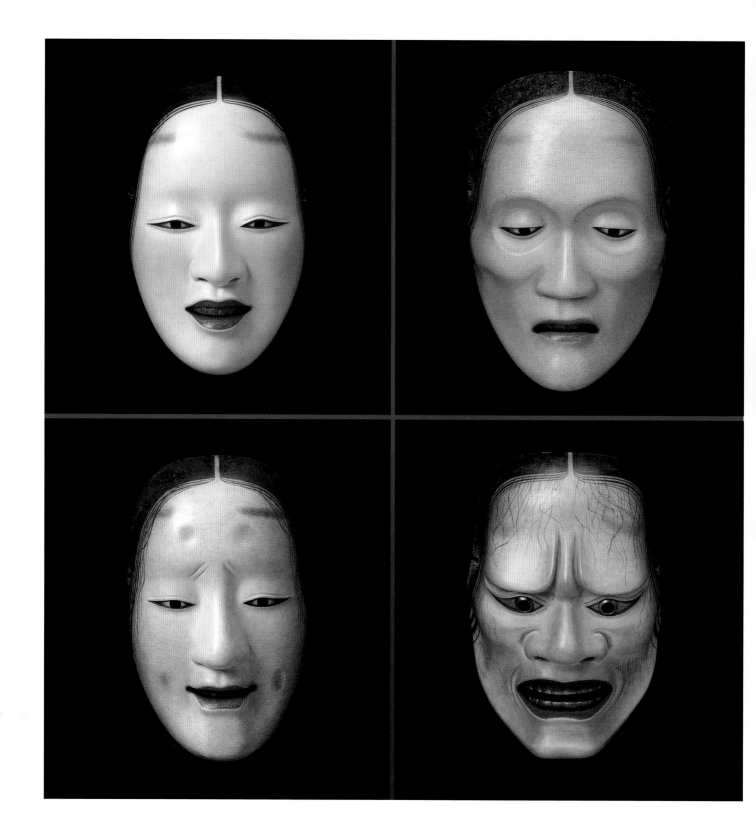

**Naki-zō** by Abe Kazuko
**Masukami** by Abe Kazuko

**Yase-onna** by Abe Kazuko
**Hashihime** by Abe Kazuko

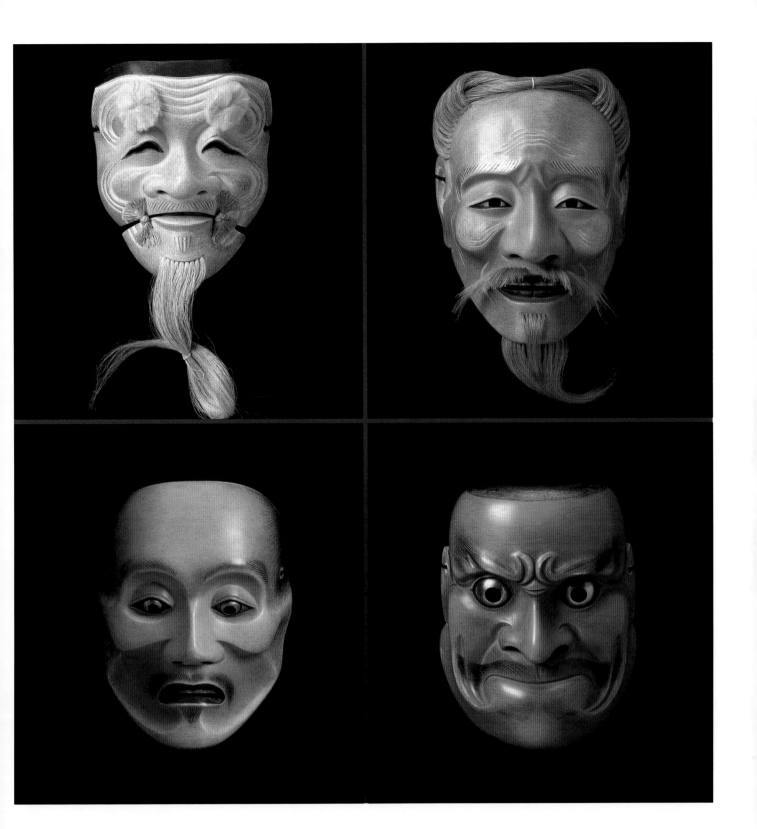

**Okina** by Abe Kazuko
**Yase-otoko** by Abe Kazuko

**Sankōjo** by Abe Kazuko
**Kobeshimi** by Abe Kazuko

# THE REPRODUCTION

## OF NOH COSTUMES

## Yamaguchi Akira

Noh, perfected during the time of the third Ashikaga shogun, Yoshimitsu (1358–1408), has evolved over time and continues this day. The Noh ideal of a spiritual consciousness, developed by Zeami Motokiyo (1363–1443), "father" of Noh, was inherited from the samurai class and carried on in ceremonial performances after the establishment of the Tokugawa government at the beginning of the 17th century. The mature form of Noh resulted from thorough study and elimination of all unnecessary elements. The term Zeami used in Motokiyo's *Fushikaden* (Teachings of the Flower), *kiwameru,* means to thoroughly study and arrive at the essential universal truths pertaining to everything. For all things, one should find the good and make it one's model. Eliminating an attitude of resistance to other people, listening to the ideas of others, and persistently pursuing a course of self-reliant study will surely lead to improvement. The greatest obstacle to such improvement is a combative pride, something every human possesses. By this, it is probably meant that one must always focus on *kiwameru* and continue the desire to learn. If I look over my 30 years spent studying Noh costumes, the importance of this attitude is something I have learned. That this has survived as food for the mind, unforgotten till today, is above all a great fortune.

Perhaps because I was brought up in the weaving workshops of the Nishijin area of Kyōto, I was not impressed with silk fabrics when I saw them. The only exceptions were the Noh costumes from the Edo period. Upon first seeing them, I was taken aback by their surprising brilliance and stood transfixed. I want to think that the Noh costumes would not let me go. Although they, too, were silk weaving, the designs and colors were not the same as others. Everything seemed different. After that, whenever I heard the words "Noh costumes", I went to wherever they were to study them. When I saw old costumes close-up, I felt something deep, distant, and different from what I felt for a kimono or an obi: question after question gushed forth. I realized that it was impossible to understand the costumes and reproduce them without knowing about Noh. In my study of Noh, I became acquainted with Satō Yoshibiko, director of the Hōshō School Instruction Committee, which supervises the management of Wan'ya bookstore, dedicated to selling books on Noh. He introduced me to the Kita school actor Gotō Tokuzō. The words of this very elderly man remain forever fresh in my heart and have served to feed a lifetime's worth of thought. He advised:

"Many Noh actors today perform in order to live. Noh has become popular, but this is bad news. Noh actors practice and practice for their own training. Then, if they make as much as three meals' worth by appearing on stage, they must be satisfied. They can hope for no more. If you research Noh costumes, do not think you can live off it. Just concentrate on your study of Noh costumes and avidly pursue your research".

OPPOSITE: The cocoons before killing their chrysalises. A camellia leaf is in the center.

When I first met Gotō, I did not know who he was, but I found him modest – to the point of wondering if he were a Zen monk- unpretentious, and refreshing. Satō Yoshihiko was the best person imaginable for guiding me as I took my first steps in the research of Noh costumes. He was a great admirer of Noguchi Kanesuke, a Hōshō actor active between the 20's and the 60's. For Satō Yoshihiko, Noguchi Kanesuke had uncovered Zeami's ideal Noh, as had the still-living Gotō Tokuzō.

As indicated above, Noh costumes reached their mature form in the mid-Edo period. This is the period in which Japanese character reached its fullest development after having being cultivated over a span of well over a thousand years

Examination of costumes: Taking measurements.

and after incorporating considerable culture from around the world. The Noh costumes, which seek an ultimate beauty held within a single object, display this spirit to its fullest. The perfection seen in Noh costumes regressed during the Meiji period as the world and the value of objects changed.

So how did I come to reproduce these Noh costumes of the 17th to 19th centuries that I had studied so exhaustively? I took pains over every aspect that seemed related to the Edo-period Noh costumes: the silkworms that produce lustrous, strong, but light threads; the techniques of reeling the thread; the methods of dyeing beautiful yarns with consideration for when the plants produce the best color and for the components and dye matter contained in each plant; the weave structure that best brings out the effect of the costume on stage and the most reliable weaving techniques to produce the structure; and the designs containing deep spiritual secrets.

There are about twenty types of Noh costumes, very few compared to the approximately 250 Noh pieces in the standard repertory. These few costume types are draped in specified ways and combined with accessories to define the various roles in each Noh performance. One might say the multiple use of a limited number of costume types in Noh is the opposite of Kabuki costumes, which are made for specific individual roles.

With Ray Associates, I investigated and analyzed over a thousand Edo-period Noh costumes, dividing them according to basics: materials, colors, weave structure, technique, and design. Learning from all the information gathered, we have brought the costumes back to life. Edo-period Noh costumes were made with the finest techniques of the time and possess great elegance. The theory, techniques and methods used to produce the world of beauty embodied in these Noh costumes cannot be replicated by modern science and technology, but must be learned through experience built up over a long time, in an approach that is rather the opposite of modern methods.

Examination of costumes: Reading the weave structure and density of warp and weft.

I felt that the most important factor in the reproduction of Noh costumes was a matter of how close I could get to the Edo period, not just in technique and environment, but also in spirit of production.

I will now discuss each aspect of the reproduction process.

### Investigation and Analysis

In order to reproduce the Noh costumes of the Edo period, one must have original costumes from the time. Through the courtesy of numerous people, we were able to visit many costume collections. When conducting the investigation, first we discarded all previous knowledge, and emptied our heads of preconceived ideas as much as

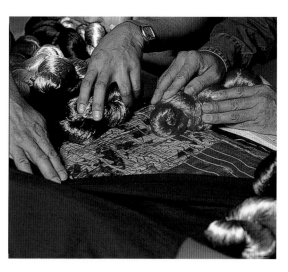

Examination of costumes: Matching the colors with those on the backside of the cloth, under the lining.

possible. This is very important for gaining honest knowledge of the vast amount of information on Noh costumes. Then, using a magnifying glass to look at the main panels, the sleeves on the front and back, the collar, and the front overlap panel, we gained some understanding of the quality and condition of the threads that were woven in the Edo period. Next we read the number of warp threads and analyzed the density of the weft threads. We measured the width of the cloth by figuring out the ground weave, by calculating how many adjacent warp threads work as a unit for the pattern weave, by discovering the style of weave, and with float weaves, by analyzing the way the warp ties are put in. Once we knew the total number of warp threads across the weaving width and the grouped harness count, we could calculate the pattern shed and only then could we begin to reproduce the patterned textile. With the colors, we analyzed the color distribution in order to figure out what the original colors were, because certain colors that we felt at first were the same often had faded differently in different areas. Then, when reproducing these differently faded colors, we decided on the shade that best enhances the stage effect when worn on a modern Noh stage. In order to understand the complete design construction, we took photographs of all parts of the costume. Finally, we placed the costume on a copy machine and recorded the design. When this was not possible, we copied it on tracing paper. We also measured each costume, but with some special exceptions, this is not important, because we always adjust the measurements of the costumes we reproduce to suit modern actors, our purpose being to make them wearable in actual performances.

### Materials

During the mid-Edo period the Japanese produced large quantities of silk thread, the raw material for most Noh costumes, and this silk thread was equal in quality to the

Chinese thread (imported from China by the Chinese, Korean, and Dutch) that had been used until then. These threads reeled from the old strains of silkworms differ greatly from threads produced by the mixed-breed silkworms of today. Great discrepancies arise from environmental variations in the places where the silkworms are raised and the thread is produced, in the climate and quality of the water, as well as in the methods used. The Edo-period threads, compared with those from modern mixed-breeds, have an extremely beautiful, lustrous sheen; the threads are thin, but strong (pure breeds 1.5-2.0 denier; mixed breeds 3.0 denier). The pure-breed silkworms, however, are weak, so their cocoons are small and the length of thread from one cocoon averages only around 500 meters (mixed-breed silkworms produce cocoons of about 1300 meters). Because the filaments of the pure-breed silkworms are thin, the proportion of broken threads during reeling is high. The best thread is reeled in spring from the live cocoons. It is easier to pick up the thread ends when reeling from live cocoons than when reeling from cocoons that have been killed and dried for storage. The length of time, and therefore the amount of silk, that can be reeled from live cocoons, however, is limited, because the chrysalis remains in the cocoon for only about two weeks before becoming a moth.

Akajuku

Seihaku

Furthermore, spring cocoons catch diseases easily, and are affected by bad weather. Consequently, fall silkworms or late fall silkworms, depending on the weather conditions, can at times produce better silk than spring silkworms.

Between hatching and spinning its cocoon the silkworm goes through five growth stages, or instars, consisting of a period of feeding followed by sleeping and shedding skin. Shedding of the skin, which happens four times, facilitates subsequent growth.

## Raising silkworms

We cultivate both spring and fall silkworms. Since 1985, I have been cultivating old, pure strains of silkworms. These strains include *akajuku, aojuku, seihaku, koishimaru, matamukashi* and *dai 'anbashi*. One year all the eggs hatched on May 26th, but while the *koishimaru* mounted the frames to begin spinning their cocoons on June 23rd, the *aojuku* mounted on the 24th, and the *akajuku* on the 26th. As a result it became clear that the different strains took different amounts of time to develop. Records show that the earlier the date in the Edo period, the longer it took to raise the silkworms. Also, if one feeds the old, pure strains highly nutritious mulberry leaves, they grow well, but produce thick thread. Presumably in the Edo period the most fertile soil was used for cultivating crops, and probably the mul-

Harvesting the mulberry leaves.

Silkworms in their fifth instar.

berry trees were grown on land unsuitable for crops but adequate for feeding the silkworms. To get accurate data, I took some of my raw silk to the Research Center for Silk Thread. When they cut the thread crosswise in order to analyze its sericin and fibroin content, the diamond blade broke on the third slice, an indication of the strength of the thread.

Raising silkworms begins with cultivating mulberry trees. Only certain types of mulberry trees are suited to feeding silkworms. The main ones used are *yamaguwa* (mountain mulberry), *hakuso* (white mulberry), and *raw* (lu mulberry). Until the 18th century the mulberry trees were allowed to grow tall, but then people started to grow them in fields, pruning them by cutting the trunks, and, thereby encouraging many low branches to spread, making harvesting easier. Mulberry trees are either propagated by planting seeds and cultivating the seedlings, or by more modem methods of grafting. The type of mulberry, the geology of the soil in which it is cultivated, and its fertility all affect the quality of the silkworm's thread. Today, the most suitable trees are *hakmo* and *yamaguwa,* both of which contain high levels of proteins and carbohydrates.

In the latter part of March we plow the soil and add fertilizer. We fertilize also after the silkworm feeding has ended in June. Then in October we build the soil by adding chopped rice stalks. Being careful not to damage the roots of the trees, we loosen the soil to allow oxygen to enter.

We start preparations for tending the silkworms when the mulberry leaves begin to appear. We clean the breeding room, and wash the various tools and sterilize them by drying them thoroughly in the sun. Ten days before hatching begins we carry all the tools, cart for carrying the mulberry leaves, shoes, and work clothes to the breeding room and sterilize them with formalin. The storage bin for the mulberry leaves inside the room is particularly important to sterilize, as it has the greatest contact with the outside. The period for growing the silkworms is adjusted to the condition of the mulberry trees, but, shortly after May 20th, we place the newly hatched silkworms in a special sterile room. We keep the temperature of the room with the young worms at 27 degrees centigrade and feed them only finely chopped leaves until the third instar. In five days the silkworm beds spread to four times their size. From the third instar we move them to the mature silkworm room. June has remarkable differences in temperature between day and night, so we warm the room at night, keeping the temperature constantly between 23 to 25 degrees centigrade. During the day we open the windows and air the room well.

Water is not good for the silkworms, so the mulberry leaves must not be wet.

When the mulberries get wet in the rain, we string a rope and hang the branches from it, and then dry them with a fan. It is thought that the more the silkworms eat, the greater the elasticity of the thread. Since an immense number of mulberry leaves are consumed at this time, it is important to make sure the silkworm beds do not get too hot. While the silkworms are sleeping one must scatter lime over the beds and line up the caterpillars. By doing this, the slow eaters will also begin to sleep.

Silkworms mounting rotating frames.

When one lays down fresh mulberry leaves, the caterpillars climb up the leaves to eat them, so the old stems must be picked out and discarded. The removal of the stripped mulberry branches and of the caterpillar's evacuations is of utmost importance in keeping the area clean. Silkworms are delicate insects that require a clean environment to grow. As is noted in old records, one must rinse one's mouth, wash one's hands and change one's clothes before entering the silkworm breeding room and proceed with the work as quietly as possible. One should designate a separate pair of shoes for wearing in the room and wear white clothes so that the dirt is immediately visible. Earth contains various bacteria and is a cause of illness spreading among the silkworms. Believing that it is humans who carry in the germs that cause diseases, we take care that mulberry branches that have come in contact with the earth are not brought into the breeding room. Naturally, cigarettes and perfume are forbidden in the breeding room, as is speaking in a loud voice. We made it a rule to change clothes between harvesting the mulberry leaves and entering the breeding room, which was bothersome, but probably one reason for our good results.

Collecting the mature silkworms.

Of all the stages, the time when the caterpillars mount the frames to make their cocoons is the most important. At this point it is essential that the breeding room is very dry. If it happens when it is raining, the quality of the silk will be bad. Also, the weather at this stage has a great effect on the way the cocoon releases its thread when reeling. From three or four days before the caterpillars mount to begin spinning cocoons, we use thermometers and fans to carefully monitor the temperature, airing the room well, and maintaining the temperature at 26 degrees centigrade. Moderated heating is a necessary contrivance for regulating the mounting.

Collecting the cocoons.

The caterpillars at the end of their fifth instar have an outstanding characteristic — they stop eating mulberry leaves and their bodies become slightly yellowish and transparent. Rising up, they sway their heads and energetically crawl around the bed. When this condition occurs, if one takes them one by one to the cocoon frames (zokumabushi> made of straw, etc.), they will spin their cocoons inside them. When the cocoon has become thinly defined, they stick their tails out and evacuate for the last time. Since this urine can soil the cocoon, one must be careful to clean it away so it does not come in contact with the cocoon. The caterpillar finishes spitting out thread in two days, and two days after that it sheds its larva skin and becomes a chrysalis, ending its tune as a caterpillar. From distributing the caterpillars in the beds to their mounting for making cocoons takes about 20 days. The number of mulberry leaves needed increases with the growth of the caterpillars, until in their fifth instar they are six times that of their fourth instar. We feed them a great deal just before they mount the frames.

### Killing the chrysalis and drying the cocoon

The hatching of the moth cuts through the cocoon threads, so to extend the reeling time beyond about two weeks, it is necessary to kill the chrysalis (*satsuyo*). Exposing the cocoons to heat is one method, but it is best not to dry out the cocoons completely. To kill the chrysalises we put them in a mud-walled, coal-heated hut for about an hour.

We judge the correct timing by placing a laurel leaf with them and watching for it to change color, the signal that time is up. This piece of ancient wisdom has been passed down through the generations of silk breeders in Azai-chō, Shiga Prefecture.

The cocoons are placed on a bamboo rack with a thick laurel leaf at least one year old on top of them. Half way through the heating, we shift the placement of the racks. This intermittent exposure to outside air affects the condition of the cocoons in subtle ways. Again, if the heat is insufficient, the moth hatches, if it is too great, the cocoon gets burnt. Once the chrysalises have been killed, the cocoons can be stored at 18 degrees for two months.

Storing the cocoons.

Reeling silk thread.

### Reeling silk thread: filature

Next we begin the process of reeling (unraveling) the threads from the cocoons. Water for this purpose should be neither tap water nor well water, but must be running water from a valley stream. Stagnant water hardens the thread; to get resilient yet soft silk thread, running water is absolutely necessary. Perhaps the difference lies in the large quantities of oxygen in running water. This, too, is a lesson from past generations based on long experience.

To reel the silk we use a foot-operated reeling tool (*zaguriki*) with two frame spools. Plenty of water is heated to 80 degrees centigrade in an aluminum pot. When bubbles slowly start to rise from the bottom, the cocoons are placed in the pot. Stirring the surface with a brush made from rice ears catches the loose ends of the silk thread. The denier (radius of the cross section) of filaments from traditional strains of silk worms differs according to the strain and feeding, but on average 10 to 12 filaments are reeled together to produce warp threads, and about 25 for supplementary pattern weft threads. In contrast, mixed strains require about 5 filaments for warp threads and between 15 and 17 for pattern weft threads. The work must be done as soon and as quickly as possible, since with every passing day the cocoon dries out further and the filaments become harder to loosen. As we consider the whiteness of the thread most important, we remove soiled cocoons and dead cocoons. We are also careful to keep the water clean at all times, changing the hot water in the pot twice during the reeling of a single spool.

### Winding the large frames

Normally we wind thread onto large frames every other day in July. On rainy days we use a dehumidifier. On days of consecutive good weather, we wind threads that were reeled in the morning onto the frames that same night. When too dry, thread reeled as singles splits up into filaments and breaks easily. On the other hand, when not dry enough, the threads stick to each other. Because the sericin in silk is a form of glue, the process of reeling these threads that are coated with sericin involves both wetting with water and drying. Once the threads have been transferred to large frames, they are left to dry naturally for about a week.

### Color: dye sources

We cultivate both safflower (*benibana*, for pink to red) and gromwell (*murasakigusa*, for purple). The first year we cultivated *benibana*, we experimented by separating fertilizers by kind and compared the growth rates of the plants. The results showed that though there was no necessity to plow very deeply, well-fertilized earth with plenty of sunlight produced the best plants.

Drying the large frames and frame spools.

Generally we plow around October, adding cow dung and rice stalks. In March we plow again, mixing in oil-cake (*aburakasu*) fertilizer. We plant the seeds in mid March. Once the first sprouts have grown to stalks about 20 centimeters long, we weed out the bed. We continue to weed until the silkworm tending ends in June soon after the safflowers bloom. For about a month, while the flowers last, we pluck the petals. Although some old records warn that picking should be done only during the early rooming hours and that rainy days are bad for harvesting, we have not found either to be true. We pluck as many bright-colored petals in full bloom as we can, when we can. We then put the plucked petals in a white cotton bag and let them sit

Plucking safflowers.

Immersing the frame spools wound with raw silk in water.

Barrels for extracting ash lye.

in water for half a day. By changing the water frequently, we leach out the yellow dye in the petals. Next we put the bag in running river water and wash out all the remaining yellow. Then we grind the petals with pestle and mortar until they condense into a compact form. This we mould into cakes (*benimochi*), which we allow to dry. We store the safflower cakes until winter, when we use them to make red dye. After harvesting the best petals, we wait till the seeds develop. Finally, we collect the seeds, pull up the plants, and distribute plenty of lime over the earth.

## Combining filaments to form thread of the right thickness

In order to create the texture of a textile, the raw silk filatures may be combined to form sturdier threads. While warp threads are given twist during this process, weft threads are not. The art of giving threads a strong twist was already known in Japan in the Yayoi period (about 200BC to 200AD) and is an extremely important factor in weaving. The warp threads used to make Noh costumes consist of several filaments plied together with 700 to 800 turns per meter.

The supplementary pattern weft threads are given no twist, but pulled to an even tension. To strengthen the threads and prevent fuzzy balls from forming, the skeins of reeled threads are placed in water for about five hours. Then they are wound from the skeins onto frame spools, and again placed in water. The amount appropriate for the piece of weaving is then wound onto rod spools. From these the thread is transferred back to the frames and allowed to dry naturally.

## Glossing with ash lye

Before dyeing the silk thread used for the pattern wefts, they are glossed, that is they have much of their sericin gum removed by simmering them in ash lye (*aku neri*). The best ash for this is taken from burnt stalks of the sticky rice (*mochigome*) plant. We place the ash in a large barrel, pour in water till the ashes are immersed in three lots, and then use the clear water on top. The raw silk threads are soaked for a whole day in the lye. They are then put in a cotton bag and heated to about 100 degrees centigrade for about an hour. The gum should be partially removed, but leaving some of the sericin coating on the threads brings out the luster when dyeing and ensures better preservation of the threads. Being organic materials, natural fibers and vegetable dyes breathe life.

## Dyeing

The method of dyeing differs depending on the characteristics of the plant used. There are specific, quite distinct methods of extracting red from safflower (*benibana*), purple from gromwell (*murasakigusa* or *shikon*) and a spectrum of shades of blue from indigo (ai), but all three are difficult to dissolve in water. For safflower, only after washing away the soluble yellow dye and adding straw ash lye that has a high alkaline content, can one squeeze out the red carthamin dye. To the purple purpurin dye in gromwell roots, one must add camellia ash lye, which is rich in alum, and acts as a mordant to stabilize and fix the color to the fibers. For indigo, the insoluble indigo blue is transformed into soluble indigo white with the aid of ash lye, lime and fermentation, then absorbed into the threads and finally reborn as indigo blue when exposed to oxygen as the threads are aired.

Dyeing.

We dye in winter, between December and February. To dye safflower, the balls of condensed petals are put in a hemp bag, immersed in straw-ash lye, and the red dye squeezed out. Repeating this four or five times produces enough for a dye bath. Even if some red dye color remains, we stop when petals turn slimy and produce oil. This is an alkaline bath with a Ph of 9 to 10. Since the dye will not take unless the bath is acid, we add rice vinegar. As the liquid approaches acid, it begins to produce carbonic acid (soda) bubbles. The threads are immersed in this and manipulated quickly so as to ensure even dyeing as the color is absorbed. The gradual disappearance of red from the dye bath indicates it has been transferred to the threads. Dyeing and rinsing are repeated to deepen the shade of red. Finally the threads are soaked in water with about two whisky shots of burnt plum vinegar (ubaiekt) added to set the color. Rinsing between dyeing removes dirt and also prevents blotchy uneven dyeing, so it is integral to the process.

The pulverized gromwell roots.

This is a digression, but one can harvest about 800 grams of dried safflower cakes from a flowerbed of about 600 square meters. To dye the same amount of thread to the same depth of color with marketed Chinese safflower requires four kilograms. In other words, our safflower is five times more potent. Again, to dye a mere 130 grams of thread a deep safflower red with Chinese safflower requires twenty kilograms. From this one can understand why safflower dyeing has been valued at a high price for so long.

For dyeing purple with gromwell, ashes from burning camellia leaves and branches are covered with water and allowed to sit. The water on top is used as a mordant to fix the color. The roots of the gromwell are immersed in water of about 60 degrees centigrade to loosen their bark. Then they are placed in a mortar and pounded with a wooden mallet so as to release the dye material. The dye lies around the roots, from which a reddish brown liquid emerges.

Rinsing the dyed yarn.

If one continually rotates the skeins in the gromwell dye, a reddish purple results. After rinsing in water, the skeins are immersed in camellia lye mordant and bit-by-bit they turn a strong bluish purple. Rinsing, dyeing, rinsing, and mordanting are repeated to produce deeper shades. To produce the slightly reddish purple used in Noh costumes, rice vinegar of a Ph 4 is added while the skeins are rotated in the bath.

Although in the Edo period the Japanese dyed indigo with *tadeai* (buckwheat), which they cultivated, we found this to be physically and technically impossible for us to do. Therefore, we dye our indigo using pellets of Indian indigo (indigo fera, *indoai*). We pound the indigo into a powder and knead it well with oil. This is dissolved in water to which caustic soda and hydrosulfide are added to make the dye bath. When the threads are immersed in this dye and rotated around they pick up a yellowish green color. When rinsed with water, this changes to a bluish green. After rinsing, when the threads are wrung dry, they become a true indigo blue. Repeated dipping produces deep shades. Since the strong alkalinity of caustic soda eats into the threads, it is necessary to rinse them very thoroughly in water.

Many different plants produce yellow, but we use phellodendron (*kihada*). The finely chopped inner bark of the phellodendron is boiled and then strained to make the dye bath. Before dyeing, the threads are prepared by steeping them in lukewarm water, after which they are immersed and rotated in the dye bath. *Kihada* is the only direct dye that is a basic dye. It has an interesting characteristic. When mixed with other dyes or when another is top dyed over it, the results are poor and a cloudy color is produced. On the other hand, when it is dyed on top of another color, the kihada aids in fixing the under dye. Top dyeing with *kihada* as the last step in dyeing safflower is particularly important. Again, yellow is top dyed on indigo to produce green. In all cases, after the final dyeing, the threads are rinsed and wrung out thoroughly and always hung in the shade.

The word for mordant (*baisenzai*) began to be used in the late 19th century. Before that mordants, which function to bring out the coloring agent and help fix the color on the cloth, were known as "helping agent" (*jōsai*) and included alum, iron, nee vinegar, plum vinegar, lime, and ash lye. The chemical composition of the ash for

Mordanting with camellia ash to produce a bluish purple.

the lye differs depending on the type of tree or straw burnt: in addition to the main alkaline substance, ash contains also small amounts of metal ions. When ash lye is used as a mordant, the trace amounts of aluminum or other metal ions play an important role. Already in the Edo period, dyers preferred to use woods containing aluminum, like camellia and mountain tea, to using straw ash when dyeing safflower and gromwell.

As mentioned before, the amount of dye color that each of the dye plants contains depends on cultivation methods and environment. The old records always mention the places of production. Until the Shōwa era (1925–1988), dye houses specialized in one color, *beniya* for safflower, *aiya* for indigo, using complex, difficult and specialized processes for each dye plant.

## Weave structure

To make *karaori*, *atsuita*, and *atsuita-karaori*, the most frequently used weave structures are 2/1 or 5/1 twills. *Hangiri*, *awase happi*, and *awase kariginu* generally are made with a 7/1 satin structure, but in the early Edo period they were woven in 4/1 satin. In the mid-Edo period, when these garments were used as stage costumes, they started to be woven with the more complex 7/1 satin structure. *Chōken*, *maiginu*, and *hitoe kariginu* are often woven in plain gauze (*ro*), where for one weft shot, every third warp thread crosses over two adjacent warp threads, and then the next three weft shots are in plain weave.

## Weaving process

**Winding threads**  The dyed skeins are wound onto frame spools. The warp threads are set aside for measuring the warp, while the weft threads are wound onto cylindrical shuttle spools. The ground weft threads for *karaori*, *atsuita*, *hitoe kariginu*, *ohōken*, and *maiginu* are immersed in water while still on their frame spools and wound onto the shuttle spools while still wet, and then again immersed in water just before weaving.

   **Warping**  The threads intended for the warp that were wound onto frame spools on the *itokuri* are measured in the right number to the right length for the cloth to be made. So as to avoid the warps crossing over each other or getting entangled, they are wound around a warping drum. The drum has a diameter of 1.5 meters and measures warps to 4.63 meters with one revolution. Since only a small multiple of ten threads can be wound onto the drum from the frame spools at one time, it is impossible to measure the whole warp, of say a *karaori* with 2580 warp ends, in one move. The drum must be rotated tens of times in order to measure the whole width necessary to make the fabric. At the end, the drum is rotated in reverse direction and the threads wound on the warp beam. The leather breaking belts on the two sides of the drum are adjusted and the warping completed by checking the tension of the threads.

   **Shuttles**  These tools for passing the weft threads through the warp shed, or opening produced by raising select warp threads and lowering others, are made of wood and metal. The center is hollowed out to hold the cylindrical spools of thread. On the side is a small hole reinforced with glass or porcelain for passing the thread end through. Larger shuttles (*tekoshi hi* or *hajiki hi*) are used for the ground wefts, while small shuttles are used for the pattern wefts.

   **Reed**  The slatted reed keeps the warp threads in line, establishing their density. It is also used to beat in the wefts as they are placed in the shed between the warps.

   **Heddles**  The heddles function to open the shed, lifting the individual warp threads that have been threaded through the holes in the heddles in an order dictat-

Jacquard loom.

Wetting the warps while weaving.

Inserting the pattern float threads.

Inserting the flat metallic paper "threads".

Brushing gelatin onto the warps.

ed by the weave structure (set-up) or in groupings that arrange the threads for weaving the pattern. The heddles are the most important element of the loom, as the heddle set-up determines the various weave structures. The process of threading the heddles begins by establishing the correct place for each string heddle by passing those that descend from the punch card apparatus on a Jacquard loom or from the upper frame (*tenshin*) on a draw loom (*sorabikibata*) through one of many small holes in a board. Next the suspended threads are tied with a thread to the wire heddles that control the pattern, and the warp threads are passed first through the central holes in the wire heddles and then through the reed.

Pattern cartoon Weaving interlaces warp and weft threads in a ground repeat and a pattern design. For this the pattern is enlarged onto graph paper as necessary. Matching the squares of the graph with the warp and weft threads, each pattern is drawn in with a different color as it creates the structure. A key to the color separation appears on the right edge of the cartoon. The weaver follows the information on the sheet when weaving in the supplementary weft threads. The units of the graph paper are calculated according to the density of the weave, so in effect the graph functions as a blueprint of the textile.

Manipulating the pattern On a Jacquard loom, the information on the design cartoon is translated to the heddles through holes in punch-hole cards. The rectangular cardboard punch-hole cards function like a computer program. Holes are punched into these cards based on an accurate reading of the design cartoon that indicates the lifting and lowering of the warp threads, a single card being equivalent to one set of weft shots. The number of cards necessary to weave one Noh costume depends on the pattern and the number of colors used. The cards are lined up horizontally and laced together with cotton strings like blinds, and then the first tied to the last so they form a circle that is set in the Jacquard structure of the loom. One after the other, the punch-hole cards touch the horizontal hooks and only those places where there is a hole does a hook pass through and pull the lead strings that put in motion the vertical heddles. As a result only the heddles connected to the particular lead strings are raised to open the warp shed for the passing of the wefts. Recently computer-operated direct Jacquards, where the pattern data is entered on a floppy disk, have become the norm and replaced the use of punch cards.

Weaving the cloth Once all the preparations described so far are completed, the actual weaving begins. Treading on a specific foot pedal on the loom sends information to the Jacquard that in turn opens and closes the sheds consecutively so the wefts can be inserted to form a pattern. It is impossible to discuss the Kyōto textile industry without mentioning climate. In order to achieve the light resilient texture of the woven Noh costumes, the warp and weft threads must be wetted during the weaving process. On dry days we also sprinkle water on the earthen floors and adjust the tension of the warps while we weave.

## Designs and motifs

Designs on Noh costumes can he roughly divided into two types according to weave set-up: double-unit set-ups (*futakoma*), where two identical patterns are set next to each other across the width of the cloth; and single-unit set-ups (*hitokama*) where a single pattern covers the entire width of the cloth. Single-unit set-ups are more complex. Again, the composition can be divided into those where the supplementary float pattern is set against a plain ground structure, and those where the supplementary float pattern plays against a ground pattern.

Tracing the designs on the Noh costumes back to their origins reveals the eager aspirations of ancient peoples. The designs are born as a means to reflect the mind: the sun, flowing water, flowers, trees, various plants and animals, man and his creations, and things beyond human control evoking the gods. By placing these textile designs on the body, does one not become enveloped in imaginary worlds filled with birds, flowers, and water?

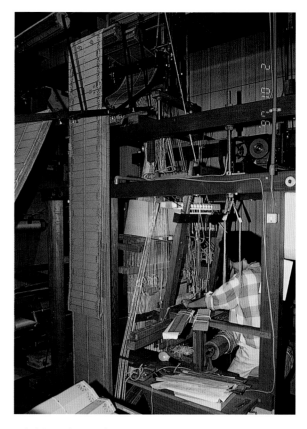

Working at the loom.

Inserting the flat gold- or silver-leafed paper "threads".

Geometric patterns derived from the aspirations of the ancient civilizations came to Japan across China from the West: from Ancient Egypt, Mesopotamia, Greece, Rome, Sassan, and Persia. On the other hand, the plant motifs that are loved and carefully nurtured by people intimate with nature are inherited from the Heian period aesthetic. While the former set of motifs are referred to generically as Chinese because of their foreign origin, the latter are thought of as peculiar to Japan.

The designs on Noh costumes are abundantly rich: set within the context of the deep themes of the Noh performances, they carry a strong spiritual character and form the criteria on which a costume is chosen. The interweaving of ground pattern and float pattern, that is the balancing against each other of geometric Chinese patterns and floral Japanese patterns, combines a bold brilliance with a delicate elegance. One might call this *yin-yang* harmony, for these opposites do not feel out of place with each other. In addition, the juxtaposition of the overall patterns of the ground with the pictorial patterns of the supplementary float give rise to a tension from which one breathes the aesthetic associated with the philosophy of Noh. Again, the composition of the designs is devised so that within the limitations of the height of the pattern unit, each rendering is skillfully varied so as to create infinite movement. For instance, a single pattern is reversed on the left and right body panels or on the sleeves and body panels, or moved in its relative position at different places, or matched with other patterns. Here, too, in the colors and color schemes one sees the spirit of Noh. ⌘

# Acknowledgments

Asami Masataka, Azai Gallery of Noh Arts, Abiko Kikuzo, Awaya Kikuo, Imai Yasuo, Umewaka Rokuro, Okami Tomoko, Ogawa Hiroshisa, Kanai Akira, Kameda Kunihei, Kagawa Yasutsugu, Kawamura Takashi, Kitagawa Zentarō, Kita Sadayo, Kirihata Ken, Kobayashi Keiko, Kondo Kennosuke, Gunter Zobel, Sasaki Hosei, Sasaki Muneo, Shiotsu Akio, Takeda Yukifusa, Tsujii Seiichiro, Tsumura Reijiro, Traditional Culture Forum, Tojo Mutsuko, Tomoeda Akiyo, Hisashi Hatsue, Horigami Ken, Honda Mitsuhiro, Homma Fusataka, Maejima Yoshihiro, Matsumoto Shigeo, Mikami Fuminori, Mikawa Izumi, Miyazaki Mitsuaki, Morita Toshiro, Monica Bethe, Yamaguchi Akira, Yamaguchi Noh Costume Research Center, Yoshikoshi Tateo, Watanabe Kyosuke, Wanami Takashi

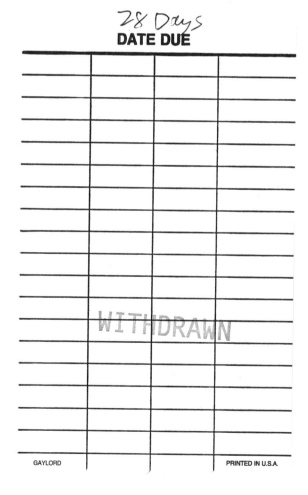